Amazing Gardens

Written by Marilyn Woolley

Flying Start
to Literacy®

Contents

What is a garden?

A garden is a place where people grow plants.

People grow all sorts of plants in their gardens. They grow grasses and shrubs, fruit trees, flowers and herbs.

People have created some amazing gardens.

Floating gardens

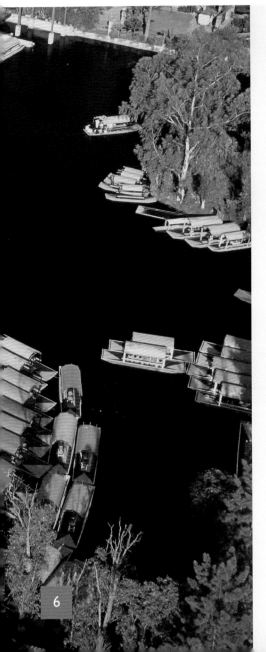

There is an amazing floating garden in Mexico. This garden was built on a lake by the Aztec people over 500 years ago.

The Aztecs dug up weeds and mud, and used them to make garden beds that floated on the lake. Then they planted vegetables in the floating garden beds.

Maze gardens

Maze gardens are puzzle gardens.

Maze gardens have tall hedges that you cannot see over or through. This means you can only see the path you are on.

The trick is to find your way into the centre of the maze and then find your way back to where you started.

Some mazes are made from corn crops.

When the corn is about ten centimetres tall, the farmers take out some of the plants to make paths. When seen from above, the mazes look like animals and other amazing shapes.

In summer, when the corn plants are tall, people visit these gardens.

Storybook gardens

This garden is full of giant storybooks.

You can visit Alice in Wonderland, sit at the table and have a tea party. And you can see Jack climbing the beanstalk.

Each storybook is made from plaster and the pages are painted in bright colours.

As you visit each part of this garden, you can listen to the stories and rhymes, too. When you pass by each part of the garden, the words come through speakers that look like rocks on the ground.

Animal gardens

This garden has plants that are grown in the shape of animals.

The plants grow on wire frames that are shaped like animals.

To make an animal, damp soil is packed
into the wire frame.

Plants with small leaves are planted
in the soil.

As the plants get bigger, they grow over
the frame. The leaves and stems are
cut to keep the shape of the animal.

Butterfly gardens

This butterfly garden is in a huge building. There are more than 3000 butterflies.

The plants in this garden provide food for the butterflies.

The temperature and the amount of mist in the air is controlled, so the plants and butterflies stay healthy.

You can walk near the butterflies in this garden. If you stay still, a butterfly might land on your hand or even your nose.

Vertical gardens

Vertical gardens are gardens that grow on walls. These gardens take up very little space on the ground. They are often found growing on buildings in cities.

The plants do not need any soil to grow. They only need a frame and lots of water.

The vertical gardens are grown because the plants help to make the air clean for people who live and work in the cities.

Another type of vertical garden is
a sky farm.

In a sky farm, different plants are grown
at each level on the building. Plants
such as lettuce, carrots, pumpkins
and eggplants are grown in sky farms.

These plants provide people with
fresh food to eat.

There are plans to build many large
sky farms in the future.

Index